A DAY ABOVE
THE EMIRATES

*Published with the support
and encouragement of
BP Middle East*

A DAY ABOVE
THE EMIRATES

By John Nowell

Published by
Motivate Publishing

Dubai: PO Box 2331, Dubai, UAE
   Tel: 824060, Fax: 824436

Abu Dhabi: PO Box 43072, Abu Dhabi, UAE
   Tel: 311666, Fax: 311888

London: London House, 26/40 Kensington
   High Street, London W8 4PF
   Tel: 0171 938 2222, Fax: 0171 937 7293

Directors:
   Obaid Humaid Al Tayer
   Ian Fairservice

First published 1994
Reprinted 1995

© John Nowell &
   Motivate Publishing 1994

ISBN 1 873544 85 5

British Library Cataloguing-in-Publication
Data. A catalogue record for this book is
available from the British Library.

Printed by Emirates Printing Press, Dubai

Contents

*Endpapers: The morning mists drape a purple haze over the Hajar
Mountains. Title page: Lush palm gardens and white sand edge the
blue-green waters of the Gulf. This page: Peaks and ridges of sand
in the giant dunes of the Liwa.*

Introduction

The United Arab Emirates is part of the Arabian Peninsula, which, in turn, forms a continental crossroads connecting Asia, Europe and Africa. It is a land of dramatic natural beauty with its turquoise seas, sand deserts, rocky plains, sabkhah or tidal flats and ancient barren mountains.

It was not always such a seemingly harsh environment. The presence of fossils of animals like early elephants, horses, hippopotami, sabre-tooth cats and others, as well as fresh-water reptiles like crocodiles and turtles, shows that the area must once have been fertile, with large, slow-moving rivers, and substantial rainfall, similar to today's African savannahs.

Early man probably arrived in the Emirates tens of thousands of years ago, and his flint tools can still be found scattered in the desert and on the edge of the mountains. The first datable evidence, however, goes back only to around 5,000BC. Shellmounds and settlements have been found along the coast and on offshore islands, indicating remains of small fishing communities that were trading up the Gulf to Mesopotamia.

The earliest large-scale archaeological remains date back to around 3,000BC to 2,500BC, about 5,000 years ago. On the slopes of Jebel Hafit and Qarn bint Saud, near Al Ain, as well as on the neighbouring Hajar Mountains down into Oman, hundreds of stone tombs from this period have been discovered, showing a sophisticated pattern of construction that could only have been undertaken by a well-organised and settled society. These people traded copper with Mesopotamia and the Indus Valley. Cuneiform tablets from the Sumerian empire refer to the import of copper from 'Magan', now identified by archaeologists as having been in the area which includes the UAE and the Hajar Mountains.

On Umm Al Nar, a small island adjacent to Abu Dhabi, the site of a port has been found that must have been a focal point of the trade, while at Tell Abraq, in Umm Al Quwain, a massive mound yielded evidence of continuous occupation from about 2,500BC to 500BC.

Other sites have been found all over the country and show the people of the Emirates in that long-off past enjoyed a sophisticated lifestyle, trading along desert and marine routes with other civilisations hundreds of kilometres away. One of the earliest records yet found of the domestication

Previous pages: East Coast sea cliffs (pages 6-7); Old palace in Wadi Hayl (pages 8-9); the dunes of the Liwa (pages 10-11).

Ceremonial fountain in Abu Dhabi.

Jebel Hafit rising above Al Ain.

of the 'ship of the desert', the camel, has been uncovered at Umm Al Nar, dating back over 4,000 years.

The great wooden dhows that line the anchorages of the Emirates today — and can be seen under construction in boat-yards around the country — are little changed from those that plied the seas from the Seventh to the Seventeenth Centuries, trading between ports from East Africa as far as China. Competition with the European powers for regional supremacy at sea throughout the late Middle Ages finally resulted in the British establishing themselves in the Gulf at the beginning of 1820, culminating in a treaty to preserve a maritime truce, and in turn earning the area yet another name, 'The Trucial States'.

For centuries, the pearl fisheries of the lower Gulf flourished; fine pearls from the Emirates were exported to India and Europe. The industry thrived during the Nineteenth and early Twentieth Centuries, providing welcome income and employment to the hardy people of the Arabian Gulf coast. However, with the advent of the Japanese cultured pearl, the pearling trade withered, leaving the people of the Emirates once more with a bleak outlook.

Progress seemed largely to pass the Emirates by during the Nineteenth and early Twentieth Centuries; indeed, one of the delights for visitors and expatriate residents is the sense of the old still to be found in the heart of modern cities. When the discovery of oil brought prosperity on a scale beyond anyone's expectations, the result was development at an accelerated pace. The first oil concession agreements with the Emirates were signed in the 1930s, but exploration did not begin until after the Second World War. The first commercial oil discovery was at Bab, in Abu Dhabi's desert, in 1958, followed by another offshore at Umm Shaif in 1959. By the beginning of the 1960s, Abu Dhabi entered the oil era, to be followed a few years later by Dubai, then Sharjah and Ras Al Khaimah.

When the United Arab Emirates officially came into being in 1971, under the leadership of the President, HH Sheikh Zayed bin Sultan Al Nahyan, Ruler of Abu Dhabi, and Their Highnesses the Members of the Supreme Council and Rulers of the Emirates, following the withdrawal of the British from the region, plans were well advanced for the creation of a modern

Flint arrowheads found in the Emirates.

Sheikh Saeed's Palace in Dubai.

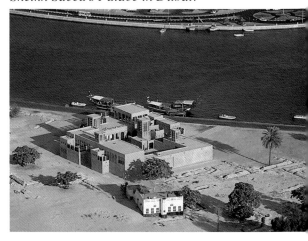

Computerised development plans.

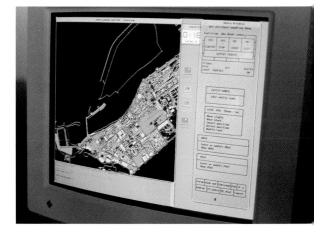

Flamingoes fly from a sanctuary.

Tree plantation in the Western Region.

nation with all the facilities and amenities its citizens would require. Since then the country has witnessed a development unparalleled by any country outside the Gulf region. Today, the country offers not only the facilities of its modern development, but also an intriguing glimpse into the history and heritage of this part of Arabia.

In recent years, interest in the UAE's environment and natural history has taken great strides forward as scientists and dedicated amateurs have found a motherlode of interest in the country's flora and fauna. Hand in hand with this interest has grown the knowledge that the fragile desert ecosystem needs special care and attention.

As preservation of the UAE's environment and wildlife has been given greater priority, so too there has come a recognition that environmental issues have a global rather than a merely national dimension. The UAE joined the Convention on International Trade in Endangered Species of Flora and Fauna, CITES, in 1990. The country is an active member of the Regional Organisation for the Protection of the Marine Environment, ROPME, along with the other five states in the Arab Gulf Co-operation Council and Iran, and has its own Federal Environmental Agency, charged with the protection of the environment and what is within it.

In Abu Dhabi, the oil companies are responsible for a number of the offshore islands, now developed as oil terminals, and for much of the desert area. They have been given the responsibility for environmental protection, and several million dollars have been spent in surveying and protecting the coast and the desert, ensuring that the industry as a whole puts the protection of the environment high on its list of priorities.

A hunting falcon.

The tangible results of environmental changes are increasingly apparent to residents and visitors alike. A simple journey from Abu Dhabi airport into the city is to drive down a mature tree-lined boulevard. Abu Dhabi is not alone in this respect; all of the Emirates are 'greening' — a fact that becomes even more apparent when viewed from the air, where the sight of gardens and plantations adds to the patterns laid down by nature thousands of years ago. The many millions of palm trees planted and carefully nurtured have changed the very atmosphere of the Emirates, so much so that many of the older UAE residents are now able to remark on the change in temperature.

The UAE is a young country with a young population, and much of the

modern recreational infrastructure is there to cater to their needs. Football is played on grass pitches, golf on grass fairways; for picnics beneath mature trees families have a choice of venue. Waterside amenities make the most of the warm and safe waters of the Gulf. The authorities are quite simply showing the lead in appreciating what nature has provided, and what can be sustained with imaginative use of water resources.

Everywhere one turns, there is ample evidence of the potential of the natural surroundings of the Emirates, and of the pleasure to be gained from an environment well tended, a point underlined by such measures as the issue of posters or postage stamps.

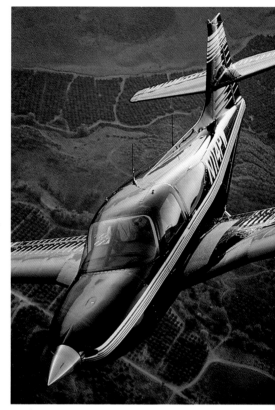

A day above the Emirates.

Preservation extends beyond the Emirates' rich natural heritage to its equally-rich cultural birthright. In an age of mass communications and global awareness, the need to preserve the cultural way of life has taken on new importance. Happily, traditions not only survive — they thrive, especially on national occasions. Music and dancing, seamanship, falconry, equestrian skills and camel lore are only a few of the leisure activities pursued energetically and in growing numbers; an early-morning drive past any of the many camel racing tracks reveals the sight of camels and riders in training.

Gardens add colour to the desert.

The influx of visitors has added further impetus to cultural preservation; the entire country is a delight for the visiting photographer. It is the blend of ancient and modern, the smiling faces, the striking architecture, the dhow-builders' yards and towering forts which combined with the delightful winter light makes the Emirates one of the most sought-after tourist destinations.

Travel broadens the mind. The modern traveller has a greater appreciation of the world than did his predecessors, and with it a keener understanding of the need to preserve the environment, the very thing that his presence threatens to destroy. Ultimately, man's future depends on this. It is not only a matter of ensuring that future generations will have material resources available. Only by developing a knowledge of the environmental principles governing the maintenance of the global ecosytem can man hope to preserve the environment sympathetically and effectively. It is to the credit of Sheikh Zayed and the people in the Emirates that a tremendous start has been made.

Dawn

6 am

After dawn prayers, friends gather near an old barasti fisherman's mosque in Abu Dhabi while a 'Pulsar' light aircraft makes a long-legged take-off into the sunrise en route to a desert rendezvous.

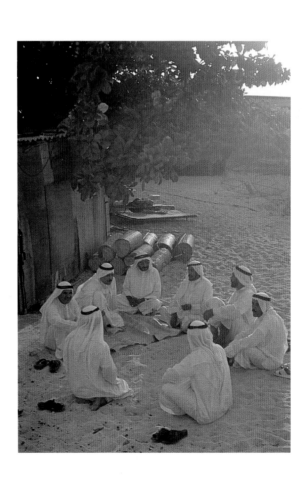

17

6.15 am

Fishermen leave the East Coast of the Emirates as the sun breaks the meniscus of the Indian Ocean. Throughout the country, men, women and children greet the new day.

18

The roaring burners break the silence of the dunes. With a sigh and a creak, the wicker basket floats free of the ground into the gentle dawn breeze — destination unknown. Balloons manoeuvre by using delicate amounts of hot air to change altitude in search of different wind direction.

6.45 am

Dubai's Creek bustles even at an early hour with traffic as 'abras', or water taxis, crisscross the waterway they share with larger craft. The Creek, which divides the city, is widely believed to be 'Cynos', the name given to the river at the lower end of the Gulf by Pliny, the Roman chronicler who described the region in the First Century AD. Peppers and coconut dry in the early morning light on a rooftop overlooking the Creek, while on the quayside, youngsters happily pose for the camera.

24

*For millennia, rain has drained off the
Hajar Mountains into the surrounding
plains; where the moisture eventually
surfaced, Al Ain oasis grew. In the date
plantations around the town, the
watering and collection of dates
continues, supply for a healthy trade in
the Al Ain souk. Along with agriculture,
Al Ain's renowned camel market makes
it a focal point for the surrounding area.
Overleaf: Plumes of dust mark the
progress of off-road adventurers on the
rocky plains of the northern Emirates.
Their destination is one of the more
remote and mountainous parts of the
country where delightful pools reward a
careful climb through rocky gorges.*

7.30 am

In Dubai Dry Docks, the largest in the Middle East, modern bulk carriers flying the flags of many nations put in for maintenance and repairs. At Port Zayed, a gas cracking tower is unloaded, while in one of the UAE's dhow building yards in Ajman, separated from the other two facilities more by time than distance, a bow drill is still used in the construction process. Overleaf: History played out in the shadow of the rugged mountains at Shams is described in fascinating detail in the Ras Al Khaimah museum, housed in the beautifully restored fort, formerly the home of the Ruling family.

8 am

Resplendent in their matching plumage, aircraft and flamingoes wheel over the clear waters of the Emirates in the early morning light, the flamingoes easily out-manoeuvring the flying machine. Millions of migrating birds stop for a rest in the many creeks and coastal lagoons of the Emirates. On Dubai's Creek, a rowboat provides a sedate crossing.
Overleaf: The passengers are enveloped in a stillness that can only be achieved in a hot-air balloon drifting on the wind, with only the distant buzz of a passing light aircraft to interrupt the calm.

33

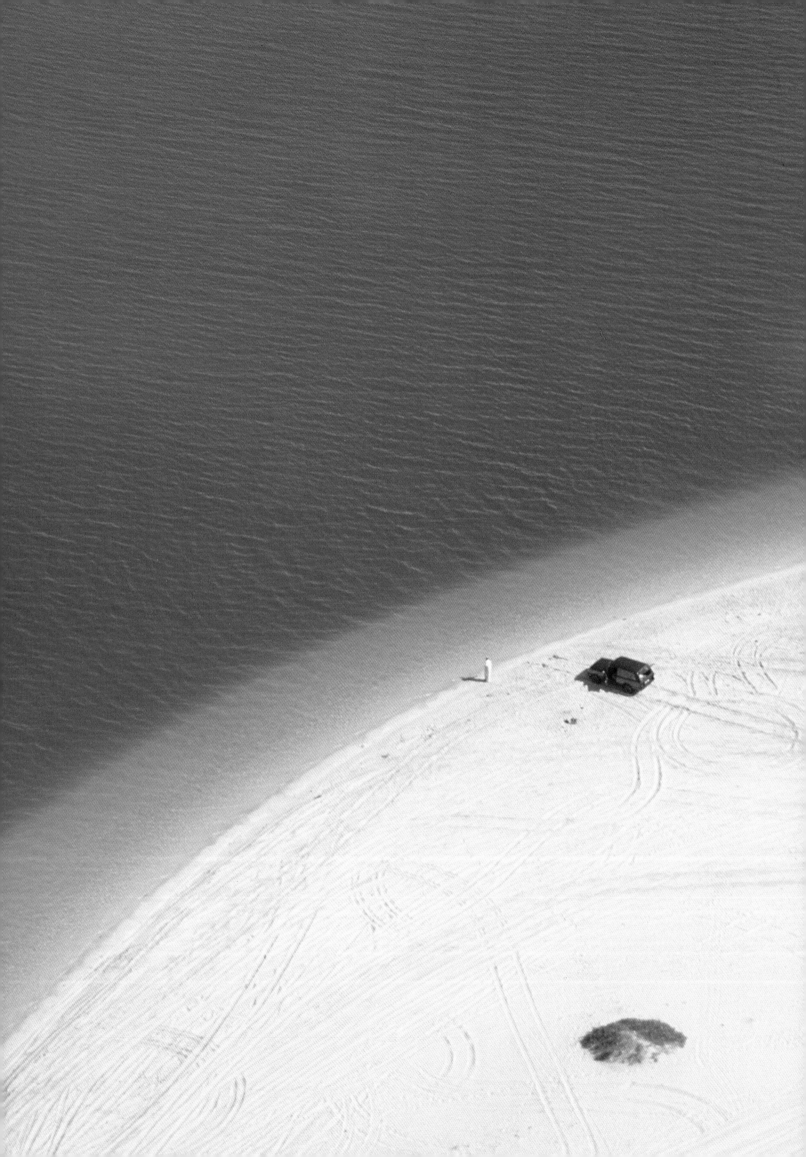

8.30 am

The clear Gulf waters are an irresistible magnet for those seeking solitude. The flag of the Emirates flies over a collection of fishing boats where nets are prepared for the next foray over the crystal clear water.

8.45 am

*What goes up eventually comes back
down again. The early-morning reverie
comes to an end; as desert gives way to
green fields, the hot air balloon slowly
and silently returns to earth, a surprise
visitor for the farm workers.*

Morning

9 am

As man encroaches, animals adapt or retreat. In the warm waters of the Gulf bordering the Emirates, the gentle dugong, once common, now exists only far to the west around the Bu Tini shoals. Dolphins frolic closer to humans — even enjoying a lift from the bow thruster of a giant tanker. Near a sand bank offshore, the adventurous don masks and flippers and join these sociable creatures in the water. In a quiet backwater far from the noise of human activity, a harmless black-tipped reef shark patrols.

9.15 am

A new park blossoms on the spit of Hamriya next to Sharjah, while endangered species also 'blossom' in captive breeding centres in Al Ain Zoo. With his keen interest in ecology, HH Sheikh Zayed bin Sultan Al Nahyan is looking for areas where the oryx can be released back into the wild. Falconing reduced the numbers of houbara significantly but now an extensive programme to redress the balance is under way, led by the Avian Research Center from its desert base near Al Ain. Overleaf: New wharfage in Dubai's Creek caters for the traditional dhow trade that has always been the life blood of commerce in the Emirates.

*The water flowing year-round over the
rocks in the Hajar Mountains is
controlled to feed the falaj systems,
carefully-designed conduits built to
carry water to terraced patches of
cultivation. The falaj systems,
introduced by Persian invaders three
thousand years ago, are augmented with
control dams and traditional irrigation
devices such as counter-weighted
buckets made of leather.*

10 am

*The UAE's elite Search and Rescue
(SAR) force prides itself on its high
degree of readiness for the task of
rescuing not only downed airmen but
also unfortunate civilians whether at
sea, in the mountains or in the desert.
The job calls for endless training to
learn and hone those life-saving skills.
Overleaf: Dubai's Victory Team, as well
as teams from Abu Dhabi Duty Free
and Abu Dhabi Aviation, have taken the
offshore powerboat racing world by
storm, applying age-old skills of
seamanship and a competitive drive
to these ultra-modern Emirates-built
'thoroughbreds'.*

10.30 am

The ever-changing skyline of Abu Dhabi's Corniche, featuring the Baynunah Tower, tallest building in the country, reflects the march of progress in the Emirates. New skyscrapers, incorporating the latest innovative architectural ideas and building techniques, dot the landscape in the capital's growing business sector.

10.45 am

At the northern edge of the Emirates are the Hajar Mountains, an area of rugged peaks and wadis shared with the Musandam area of Oman. These mountains are the traditional home of the Shihuh, a tribe about which much is rumoured but comparatively little is known. Many of the mountain men of Ras Al Khaimah still carry a little axe which was once a weapon but now serves as part of the formal dress. Modern facilities have been provided for these hardy people in the lower valleys, but some still prefer to eke out a living high in the mountains.

11 am

The urge to zoom across the sky or water can be satisfied throughout the year in or above the warm waters of the Gulf. Every imaginable variety of sport is enjoyed, including para-sailing, with professional guidance for all ages.

Once just a landmark on the track between Dubai and Abu Dhabi, Jebel Ali has lent its name to a remarkable port — with the Great Wall of China, one of only two man-made features visible from outer space — and Free Zone that are the envy of the rest of the world. The development was part of the far-sighted plan for the future mapped out by the late HH Sheikh Rashid bin Saeed Al Maktoum, architect of modern Dubai. HM Queen Elizabeth II opened the Free Zone in 1979, signalling the completion of the gargantuan task of excavating millions of tons of earth to form the world's largest man-made harbour. Since it opened, more than 625 companies have set up operations in the zone, with more being added daily.

A trading dhow makes stately and steady headway on its voyage toward the Strait of Hormuz and beyond. For other working boats, duties of state give respite to the daily push and pull as they stand by to give a genteel push to a visiting Royal Yacht whose arrival is heralded by bunting-clad dhows carrying traditional bands.

11.45 am

The flags of the six members of the Arab Gulf Co-operation Council – Bahrain, Kuwait, Oman, Qatar, Saudi Arabia and the UAE – proudly fly from the ceremonial fountain beneath the Inter-Continental Hotel in Abu Dhabi. In the desert, a hand-held Global Positioning System computer allows travellers to determine their exact position – in this case, an unmarked dune at Qusaihwira, near the southernmost point in the UAE. Overleaf: At an old palace in Wadi Hayl in Fujairah, the slightest movement of air would provide a cooling breeze. On the coastal plain, the great castle of Fujairah marks a time not that distant when every town and village needed its defensive strongholds.

Mid-day

68

12.30 pm

The commanding position of the fort at Bithna gave it control of a strategic route through the Hajar Mountains. Square forts were both dwellings and fortresses, entered through a door at the base and with rifle holes in the upper floors. The 'pepper-pot' towers, usually positioned on high ground for good defensive visibility, had access high off the ground only by rope ladders which could be easily withdrawn.

Previous pages: 'Snoopy Island' off the coast of Fujairah is a favourite site for snorkelling and diving.

12.45 pm

*The evidence of long-vanished warriors
is etched on rocks in the mountains
while at Tell Abraq, in Umm Al Quwain,
a massive mound holds more clues to
the past. Excavations revealed traces of
continuous occupation from 2500BC to
500BC when the shoreline altered. Also
rescued from oblivion is an indigenous
hedgehog which fell into a falaj and was
saved by a member of the Emirates
Natural History Group.*

1 pm

When occasional winter storm clouds obscure the Hajar Mountains, even military helicopters return to base to escape the impending rain. Against the backdrop of the Abu Dhabi Corniche, a Bell helicopter of Abu Dhabi Aviation carries oil workers on a never-ending shuttle between offshore platforms and home base.

1.15 pm

The perpetual spring water from the Hajar Mountains enabled Bronze Age settlers to establish a village at Bidiya over 4,000 years ago. Today, the oldest mosque still in use in the UAE stands at the same location on the East Coast. Known as the 'Ottoman Mosque' in a time-twisted reference to its builder, Othman, the mosque nestles into a hillside near the coast and is distinguished by four small domes supported by a massive central pillar.

1.30 pm

A fishing boat races across crystal waters, clear testimony to the effectiveness of pollution control measures necessary for a country whose coastline borders busy shipping lanes. On the East Coast, a post-lunchtime calm settles over the fishing village of Sharm.

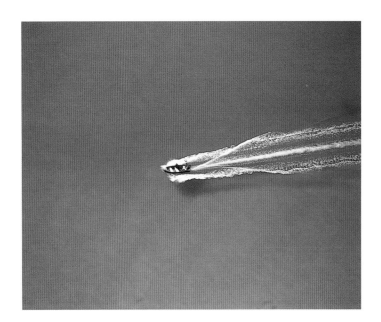

1.45 pm

Archaeologists investigating sites in Ras Al Khaimah may have located the ancient site of Julfar, a major point on the ancient trade routes between the Indus Valley and Mesopotamia. In the mountains behind Julfar, pictographs show warriors on horseback.
Overleaf: The semi-circular curve of a shore-anchored net is kept under careful guard by a fisherman in his boat. Onshore, compatriots pull the net in to beach their rich haul of fish.

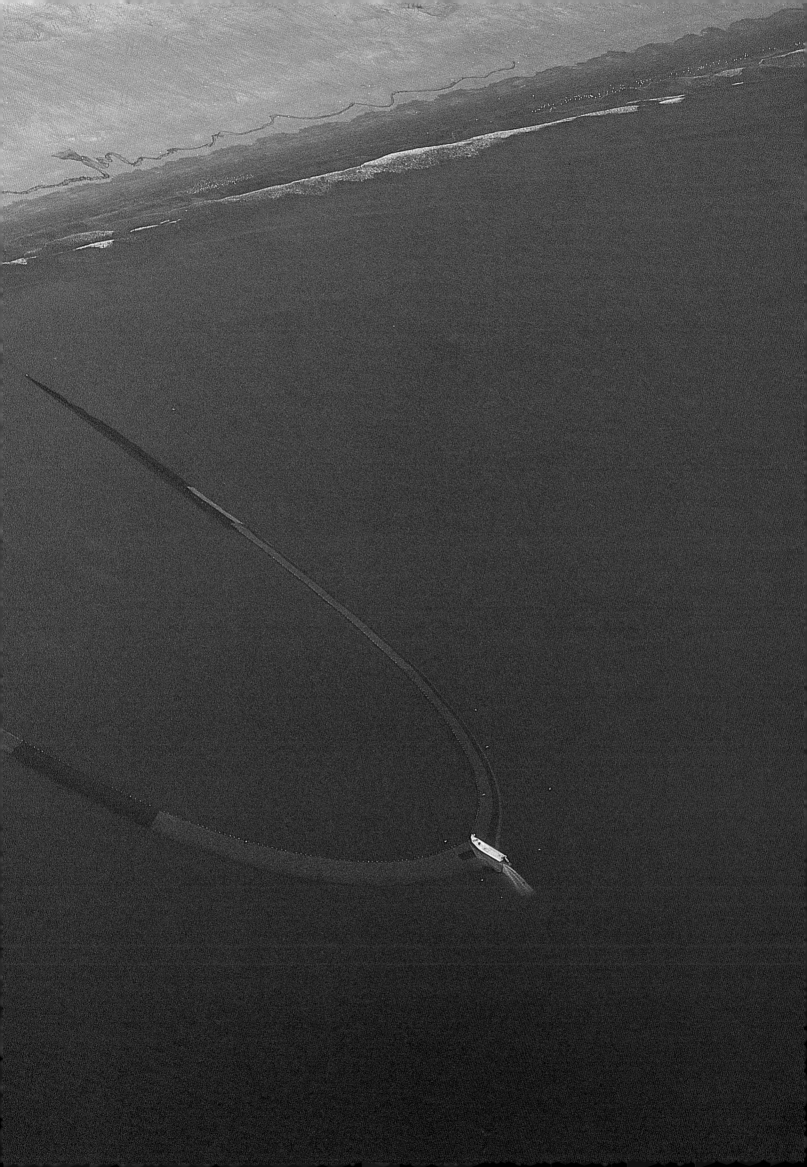

2.15 pm

The fort at Umm Al Quwain is built in the classic style, a rectangle with circular towers. Beneath the verdant palm trees, brass-wheeled cannons bear witness to a defensive position from days past.

2.30 pm

Traditional sailing dhows gather at the starting point some 50 miles west of Abu Dhabi, ready for the big race. The signal is given, their distinctive lateen-rigged sails billow in the wind and all across a sparkling sea, the boats surge forward — the race is on!

The sheer exhilaration of laughing riders on galloping horses shows the lasting importance of Arab horses. Ancient coins depict the Ruler holding a horse in the palm of his hand, a clear indication that the horse was valued above all other possessions. Today, many equestrian clubs have been established around the Emirates with breeding programmes aimed at preserving true Arab bloodlines.

3 pm

Gazelles romp across a mosaic desert on the bottom of the Al Ain Palace Hotel pool, recalling the origins of Abu Dhabi. History tells of bedu hunters who followed a gazelle to a fresh-water spring on a coastal island. Such was the value of this water source that a fort was built to protect it. The community that developed around the fort was called Abu Dhabi, meaning 'Homeland of the Gazelle'. The fort, after serving as home to the Ruling family, has been restored and turned into the UAE Centre for Documentation and Research.

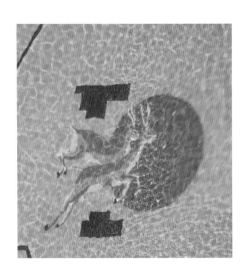

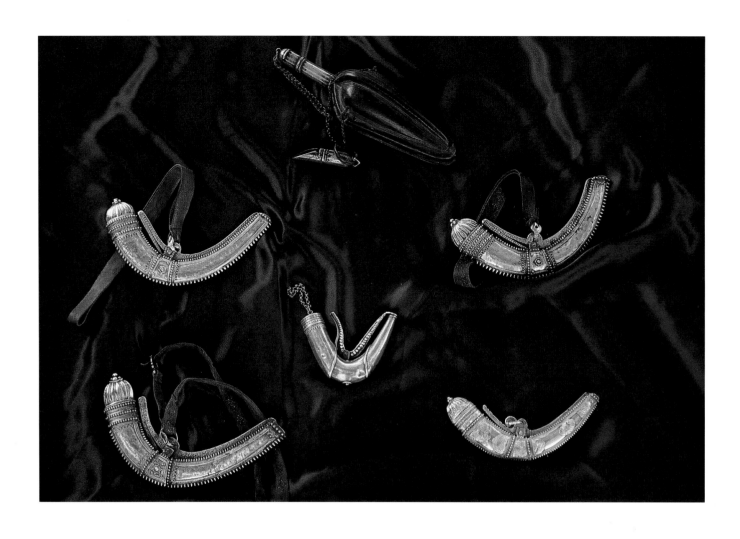

3.15 pm

Beyond landscaped islands, rainbows and dhows is the architectural landmark of the Sharjah Souq, a veritable Aladdin's cave of both modern merchandise and antiques. Popular relics of the past include powder flasks, dating from the days of flintlock firing mechanisms and the traditional 'khanjar' or dagger. Now rarely worn in the Emirates except on ceremonial occasions, a khanjar is a treasured possession of the average family as well as a work of art in its own right with its finely decorated handle and silver-wound scabbard.
Overleaf: Booms arched under the strain of their massive sails, the racing dhows vie for position.

3.45 pm

The Abu Dhabi Corniche provides a splendid backdrop for traditional dancing, a cultural display to celebrate special occasions and public holidays. While the men dance the 'Ayalah', waving their golden swords or canes, young ladies swing their hair in the graceful movements of the 'Na'asha'. Overleaf: Hilltop ruins at Dhayah recall a four-day siege by British forces in 1819 which led to the signing of a peace treaty in 1820.

4.15 pm

A long finger of high sand dunes protected the old creek of Ras Al Khaimah through the centuries. Today the modern town forms the barrier to the open sea but the traditional trading dhows are still very active. Near Rams, a youngster waves a greeting from the vantage point of his platform built to catch the faintest of breezes.

4.30 pm

By now, two clear leaders have emerged from the massed start and begin to pull clear away in front.
Overleaf: A towering fountain of spray in the centre of Sharjah lagoon makes a permanent focal point while the arrival in Sharjah Creek of a boat-load of stuffed lamb from Yemen creates a moment of excitement.

5 pm

*The sweeping curve from the
Al-Garhood Bridge encloses the
undulating fairways and greens of the
Dubai Golf and Yacht Club. Designed
for sport, this modern feature of water
and greenery also provides a welcome
new habitat for migrating birds. Seen
from a different angle, the man-made
mounds resemble the drumlins laid
down by glaciers.*

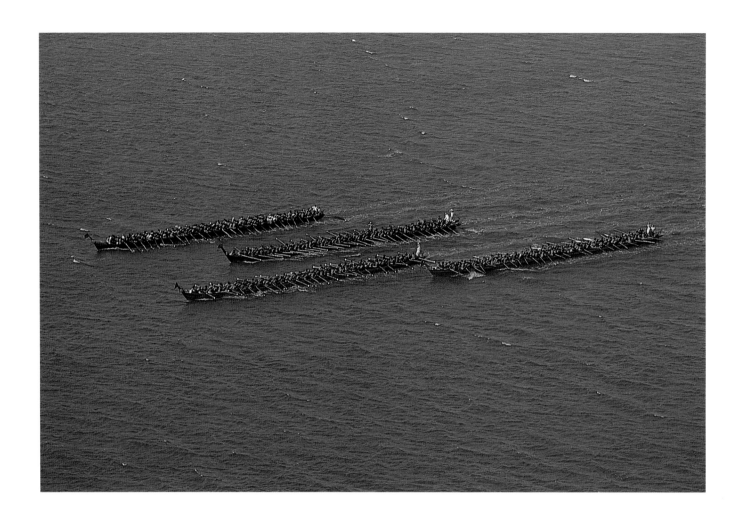

In bygone days, the long pearling season ended with the fleet upping anchor and racing for home. Inspired by this, long rowing boats race across the water off the Corniche in Abu Dhabi in one of a series of races which attract competitors from all around the Gulf. Building these sleek craft keeps a major part of the Emirates' traditional boat building industry busy.

5.30 pm

Traditions run deep in the Emirates. Though pearl trading has declined, and pearl diving is but a memory, dhow building continues to thrive in Ajman, Abu Dhabi and Dubai. The traditional sport of falconry flourishes. In an Al Ain souq, old weapons and crude bullets have achieved the status of antiques and souvenirs.

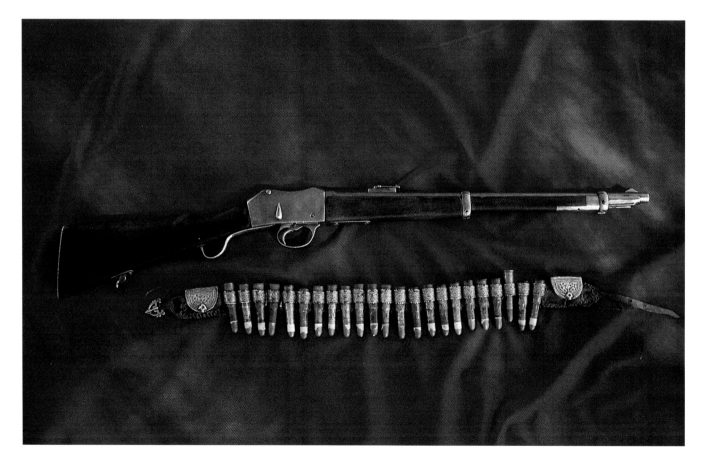

The newly-restored Dubai Fort, next to the Ruler's office by the Creek, is once again a focal point of the city. Despite being surrounded by modern buildings and busy traffic, inside is a haven of tranquillity offering an insight into the old way of life – even a working wind-tower. Museum galleries offer a different view of the dhow which can be seen from below 'floating' on blue glass.

Evening

*Dhows on a silver sea crowd through
the Corniche channel. The jubilant
winning crew, now out of the wind, pass
slowly in front of the reviewing stand.*

6.15 pm

In the Emirates, coffee is more a social occasion than a means of slaking the thirst. Coffee beans are roasted and ground before being added to a pot. The traditional coffee pot, a 'dalla', is crafted from silver, bronze or copper in a variety of designs. By studying the patterns and craftsmen's stamps, experts can identify not only who made a particular dalla, but also in which region of the Arabian Gulf it was made. With the extensive trading throughout the region, coffee pots from different countries could be seen in villages far from their original home. The local sugarless Arab coffee is flavoured with cardamom and served in a little cup called a 'fingan'.

6.30 pm

The UAE is one of the world's leading camel-breeding centres, maintaining advanced facilities dedicated to the study of camels. Veterinarians from around the world visit regularly to study and observe.

6.45 pm

Rowing boats return across a golden sea. The soft evening light casts its glow on the restored Sheikh Saeed's Palace in the curve of Dubai's Creek at Shindaghah where excavations are uncovering foundations of some of the city's other original buildings. Overleaf: Camel-riding among the big red dunes near Al Ain gives visitors a taste of Arabia.

7.30 pm

*The last horizontal rays of the setting
sun are reflected from the towering
landscape of the Abu Dhabi Corniche.
The same light picks out a solitary
stroller on one of the many beaches
in Sharjah.*

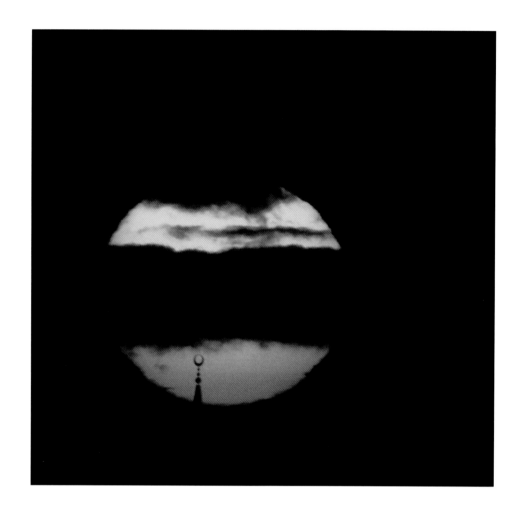

8 pm

*As the crescent of Islam is silhouetted in
the last light of day, the minarets and
domes of one of the many beautiful
mosques in Abu Dhabi reflects the
afterglow of the sky.
Overleaf: A microlight aircraft returns
to make a final landing at an airstrip in
Umm Al Quwain.*

Author's acknowledgements

Aerial photography demands more of the person controlling the aircraft than of the person holding the camera. Here in the Emirates, where general aviation is actively encouraged, I have been fortunate in having flown and worked with top-notch aviators of all nationalities. They include, from Abu Dhabi Aviation, Captains Jeremy Railton, Ernst Maas, Wayne Frankland and Ahmed Rashid; from AeroGulf, Captains John Kirk, Peter Spoor, Kevin Gray, Steve Johnson, engineers Phil Mortimer and Geoff Dentith and special thanks to Captain Alan Parsons; from the UAE Air Force, Lt Col Rashad Al Saadi, Majors Hassan Attar, Abdullah Al Hashmi, Ameen Al Jonaibi, Mohammed Al Khatery, Sultan Matar Al Senani, Sultan Rashid Al Shamsi, Ahmed Al Taboor and Raja Saleem, Captains Ali Obaid Al Khadar, Ateeq Tarish Al Qubasi, Ashoor Al Mullah, Hassan Al Hamar, Nofal Al Awani and Salim Al Kayoumi; from Fujairah Aviation Centre, Khalid Masood Butt, David Hopkins and special thanks to Tom Brown; from general aviation, Adel Al Otaiba, Rodus Adam, Mike Alexander, Maurice Barnes, Paul Bramham, Graham Bunn, Donnie Ditty, Tony Duggan, Mick Dunn, Graham Finch, Douggie Gibbons, Geoff Gladstone, Ron Hinchey, Stuart Hughes, Francoise Hochart, Graham Jackson, Allan King, Dr Ron McCulloch, Lester Mcilwaine, Charles Martin, Chris Miller, Andy Nettleton, Jonathan Pettman, Ulf Preisler, Majed Rafah, Charlie Rathbone, Jim Ross, Captain Riaz and all the instructors of Emirates Flying School, David Roseblade, Glyn Rowlands, Tim Seabrook, Richard Stockdale, Alan Teisseire, Crawford Turner, David Young, and finally, the ladies, Jane Willis, Jane Stewart, Patricia Williamson, Susan Carden and all the 'balloonatics'.

My thanks to Lt Col Ali Al Mansoori, Major Salem Al Zahmi and Captain Meshal Al Dhanni whose efforts made the dhow race pictures possible.

Special thanks to Frank Hughes, Alex Johnston and 'Smokey' Furness, three of the unsung heroes who fly in the back of helicopters and do all the hard work of rescuing people while the pilots sit in relative comfort up front.

I have enjoyed the companionship of fellow photographers Roz Buckton, Ron Codrai, Dave Drinkwater, Alan Ewens, Connie Eide, Rob Jennings, Ali Hassan Kreidie, Mike Reader and Charles Alphonso of Prolab, Bernie Reilly, Mike Shepley, Antonio Skepis, Jean-Louis Hissette of Maps Geosystems, Ron Thibedeau, Charles Turner and Paul Woodland.

My thanks to Mohammed Suwedi, Salem Al Qubassi and Abu Ameer of Abu Dhabi Municipality; Rodney Bogg of Dubai Creek Golf and Yacht Club; Chuck Grieve and Warren Jackson of Motivate Publishing; Nail Sohoglu and David Nicholson of the Chicago Beach Hotel; Saif Sultan, Allan Dinnadge and Christine Igoe of Jebel Ali Free Zone; and Trevor McKeown of Gulf Cobla.

Members of the Natural History Groups in the Emirates have been a great source of inspiration, especially Peter Hellyer, Jim Footit, Wanda Barnes, Carolyn Lehman, Charles LeBach, Kate and Roger Osborne and guest speakers; Professor Dan Potts from the University of Sydney, Peter Whybrow, Natural History Museum, London and Dr Geoffrey King, London University.

Special thanks to two individuals who actively encourage others to learn to fly and participate in general aviation. The first, Sheikh Hussein Al Moalla, gives much of his own time to encourage people of all walks of life to enjoy flying. The second, Sheikh Mishal Yousef Al Sabah, is one of the few people in the world who is actually keeping general aviation alive by building new light aircraft.

My heartfelt thanks to my children Marc, Kerri, Robert, Simone, Nicholas and William and my wife Christine who, although they are scattered across three continents, continue to give their support by achieving A grades and Honours degrees.

And finally, my thanks to BP Middle East, whose support and encouragement made the publication of this book possible.

Arabian Profiles
edited by Ian Fairservice and Chuck Grieve

Land of the Emirates
by Shirley Kay

Enchanting Oman
by Shirley Kay

Bahrain – Island Heritage
by Shirley Kay

Kuwait – A New Beginning
by Gail Seery

Dubai – Gateway to the Gulf
edited by Ian Fairservice

Abu Dhabi – Garden City of the Gulf
by Peter Hellyer and Ian Fairservice

Sharjah – Heritage and Progress
by Shirley Kay

Fujairah – An Arabian Jewel
by Peter Hellyer

Portrait of Ras Al Khaimah
by Shirley Kay

Gulf Landscapes
by Elizabeth Collas and Andrew Taylor

Birds of Southern Arabia
by Dave Robinson and Adrian Chapman

Falconry and Birds of Prey in the Gulf
by Dr David Remple and Christian Gross

The Living Desert
by Marycke Jongbloed

The Living Seas
by Frances Dipper and Tony Woodward

Mammals of the Southern Gulf
by Christian Gross

Seafarers of the Gulf
by Shirley Kay

Architectural Heritage of the Gulf
by Shirley Kay and Dariush Zandi

Emirates Archaeological Heritage
by Shirley Kay

Sketchbook Arabia
by Margaret Henderson

Storm Command
by General Sir Peter de la Billière

Looking for Trouble
by General Sir Peter de la Billière

This Strange Eventful History
by Edward Henderson

Juha – Last of the Errant Knights
by Mustapha Kamal,
translated by Jack Briggs

Fun in the Emirates
by Aisha Bowers and Leslie P Engelland

Fun in the Gulf
by Aisha Bowers and Leslie P Engelland

Mother Without a Mask
by Patricia Holton

Zelzelah – A Woman Before Her Time
by Mariam Behnam

Premier Editions

A Day Above Oman
by John Nowell

A Day Above the Emirates
by John Nowell

Forts of Oman
by Walter Dinteman

Land of the Emirates
by Shirley Kay

Abu Dhabi – Garden City of the Gulf
by Ian Fairservice and Peter Hellyer

50 Great Curries of India
by Camellia Panjabi

MOTIVATE
PUBLISHING

The Thesiger Library

Written and photographed
by Wilfred Thesiger:

Arabian Sands

The Marsh Arabs

Desert, Marsh and Mountain

My Kenya Days

Visions of a Nomad

The Thesiger Collection
a catalogue of photographs
by Wilfred Thesiger

Thesiger's Return
by Peter Clark
with photographs by Wilfred Thesiger

Arabian Heritage Guides

Snorkelling and Diving in Oman
by Rod Salm and Robert Baldwin

The Green Guide to the Emirates
by Marycke Jongbloed

Off-Road in the Emirates
Volumes 1 & 2
by Dariush Zandi

Off-Road in Oman
by Heiner Klein and Rebecca Brickson

Beachcombers' Guide to the Gulf
by Tony Woodward

Spoken Arabic – Step-by-Step
by John Kirkbright

Arabian Albums

Written and photographed
by Ronald Codrai:

Dubai – An Arabian Album

Abu Dhabi – An Arabian Album

**The North-East Shaikhdoms –
An Arabian Album**

Travels to Oman – An Arabian Album